BUILDING THE WAY TO HEAVEN

The Tower of Babel and Pentecost

BUILDING THE WAY TO HEAVEN

The Tower of Babel and Pentecost

MAURA ROAN MCKEEGAN

Illustrated by T. Schluenderfritz

EMMAUS ROAD
PUBLISHING

Steubenville, Ohio
www.emmausroad.org

Emmaus Road Publishing
1468 Parkview Circle
Steubenville, Ohio 43952

© 2018 Maura Roan McKeegan
All rights reserved. Published 2018
Printed in the United States of America

Library of Congress Control Number: 2018937275
ISBN: 978-1-947792-77-7

Unless otherwise noted, Scripture quotations are taken from The Revised Standard Version Second Catholic Edition © 2006 by the Division of Christian Education of the National Council of the Churches of Christ in the United States of America. Used by permission. All rights reserved. The Revised Standard Version of the Bible: Second Catholic Edition was published in 2006 with ecclesiastical approval of the United States Conference of Catholic Bishops.

Design and Illustrations by:
T. Schluenderfritz

Nihil Obstat: Rev. James M. Dunfee, Censor Librorum
December 14, 2016

Imprimatur: Jeffrey M. Monforton, Bishop of Steubenville
December 14, 2016

The nihil obstat and imprimatur are declarations that work is considered to be free from doctrinal or moral error. It is not implied that those who have granted the same agree with the content, opinions, or statements expressed.

Building the Way to Heaven
The Tower of Babel and Pentecost

Maura Roan McKeegan

Illustrated by T. Schluenderfritz

Have you heard of the Tower of Babel?
Do you know about Pentecost, too?
One is from the Old Testament,
One is from the New.
Both stories are the Word of God,
Their messages are true;
But when you see them side by side,
A hidden part comes through.

Now take a closer look
At how their histories are told:
See the Holy Spirit work
As mysteries unfold.
Find the buried treasures
That the Sacred Scriptures hold;
Let the New unlock the door
To secrets of the Old!

"The New Testament lies hidden in the Old, and the Old is unveiled in the New."
—Saint Augustine

You might have heard the story
Of how Noah built an ark
And the whole earth was covered in water.
After that Great Flood,
No one was left on the earth
Except Noah's family.

You might have heard the story
Of how Jesus rose from the dead
And the whole earth was covered in His mercy.
After Jesus ascended into heaven,
His people remained on the earth
And formed a new family of Christians.

Noah's children grew into many nations
And spread out over the earth.
The whole world spoke the same language.
They used the same few words.
Some of Noah's descendants traveled
From the east
To live in a land called Shinar.

God's children came from every nation
Under heaven.
The whole world spoke different languages.
They used different words.
The Apostles traveled
From Mount Olivet, where Jesus ascended,
To dwell in a nearby city called Jerusalem.

The people of Shinar
Wanted to make a name for themselves
So that they would not be scattered all over the earth.
They decided to build themselves a city
And a tower with its top in the heavens.

The Apostles in Jerusalem
Wanted to make the name of Jesus
Known all over the earth.
Jesus told them to remain in the city,
To wait for a promise from His Father in heaven.

One day, the people of Shinar
Began making bricks
For their city and their tower with its top
In the heavens.
They baked the bricks in fire,
And the Lord came down from heaven
To see what they had built.

One day, the Apostles
Were gathered in a house
When suddenly a sound like the rush of a mighty wind
Came from heaven.
Tongues of burning fire
Came down from heaven
To rest on each one of them.

The tower was going up
And the Lord saw that the people were filled with pride.
God said this was only the beginning
Of what the people would do.
But they were doing it to make their own name known.
So God went down
And confused their language
So that they would not understand one another's speech.

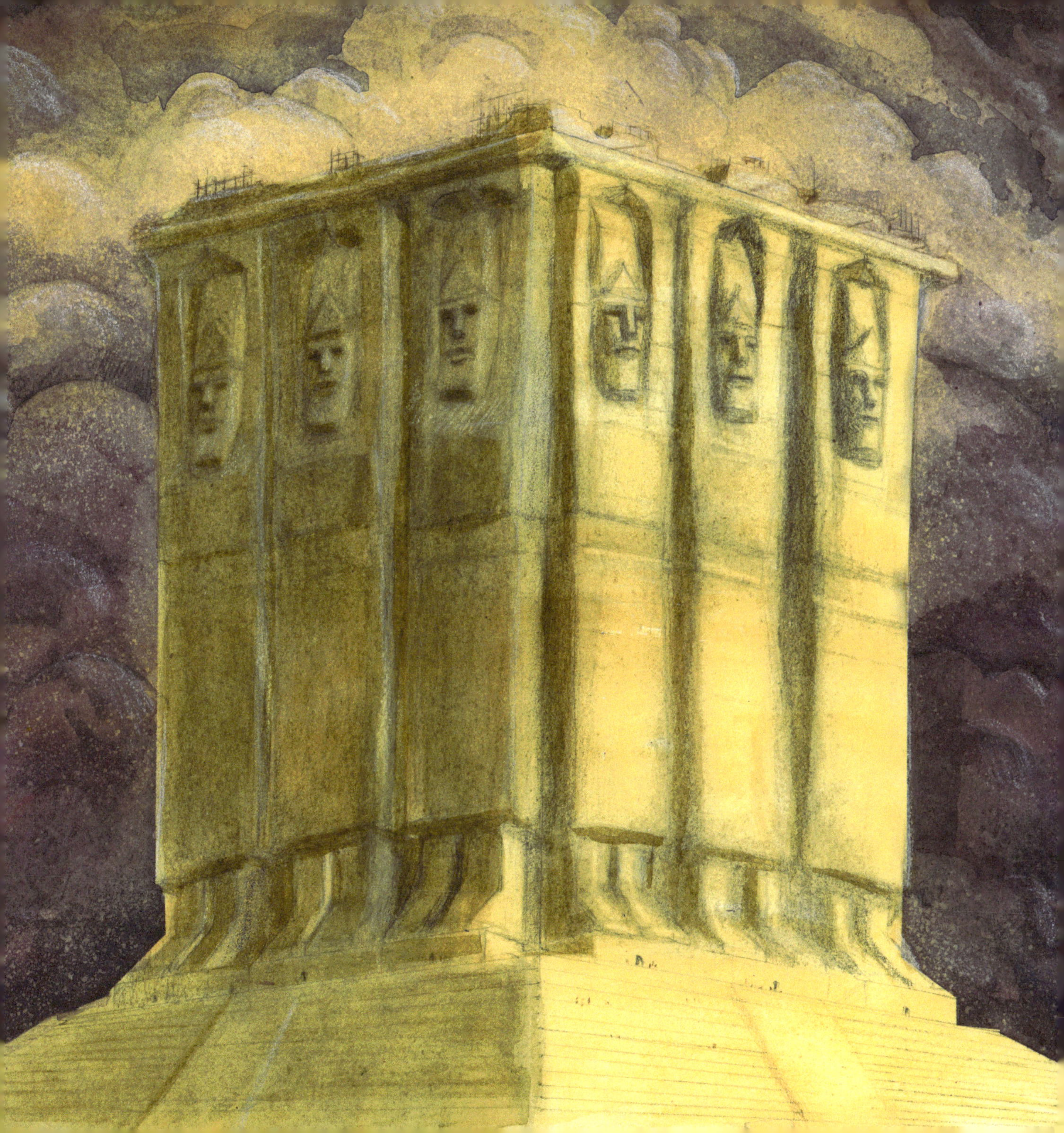

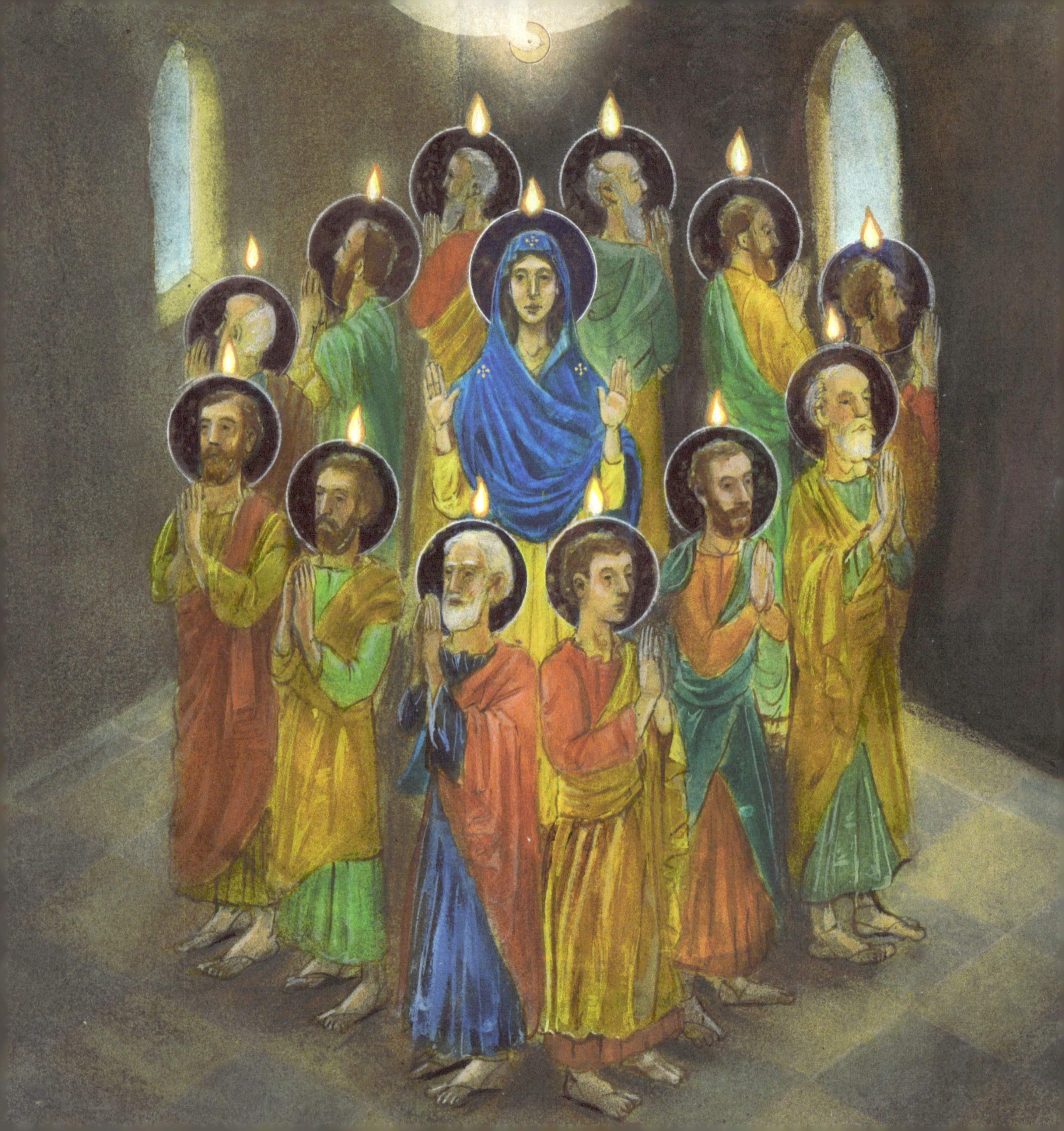

The fire came down
And the Apostles were filled with the Holy Spirit.
This was only the beginning
Of all the Apostles were about to do
To make the name of Jesus known.
The Holy Spirit came down
And gave them a miraculous language
So that all who heard them would understand their speech.

The people of Shinar stopped building their city
And the place was called Babel
Because there the Lord confused the language of the whole earth.
And from there, He scattered the people all over the earth.

When the Apostles spoke, the people in Jerusalem
Were bewildered and amazed,
Because each one heard them in his own native language
Though they came from every nation under heaven.

After God came down to Shinar,
No one spoke the same words anymore.
They could not understand each other's languages.
The people lost their city,

And the Tower of Babel
Never reached from the earth
Up to the sky.
With the stones they made,
The people could not build
Their own way to heaven.

After the Holy Spirit came down on Pentecost,
The Apostles spoke in other tongues.
Every person understood them in his own language.
The Apostles proclaimed the city of God,
The heavenly Jerusalem,
Reaching from the sky
Down to the earth.
Jesus, the cornerstone,
Had come to build
The way for His people to reach heaven.

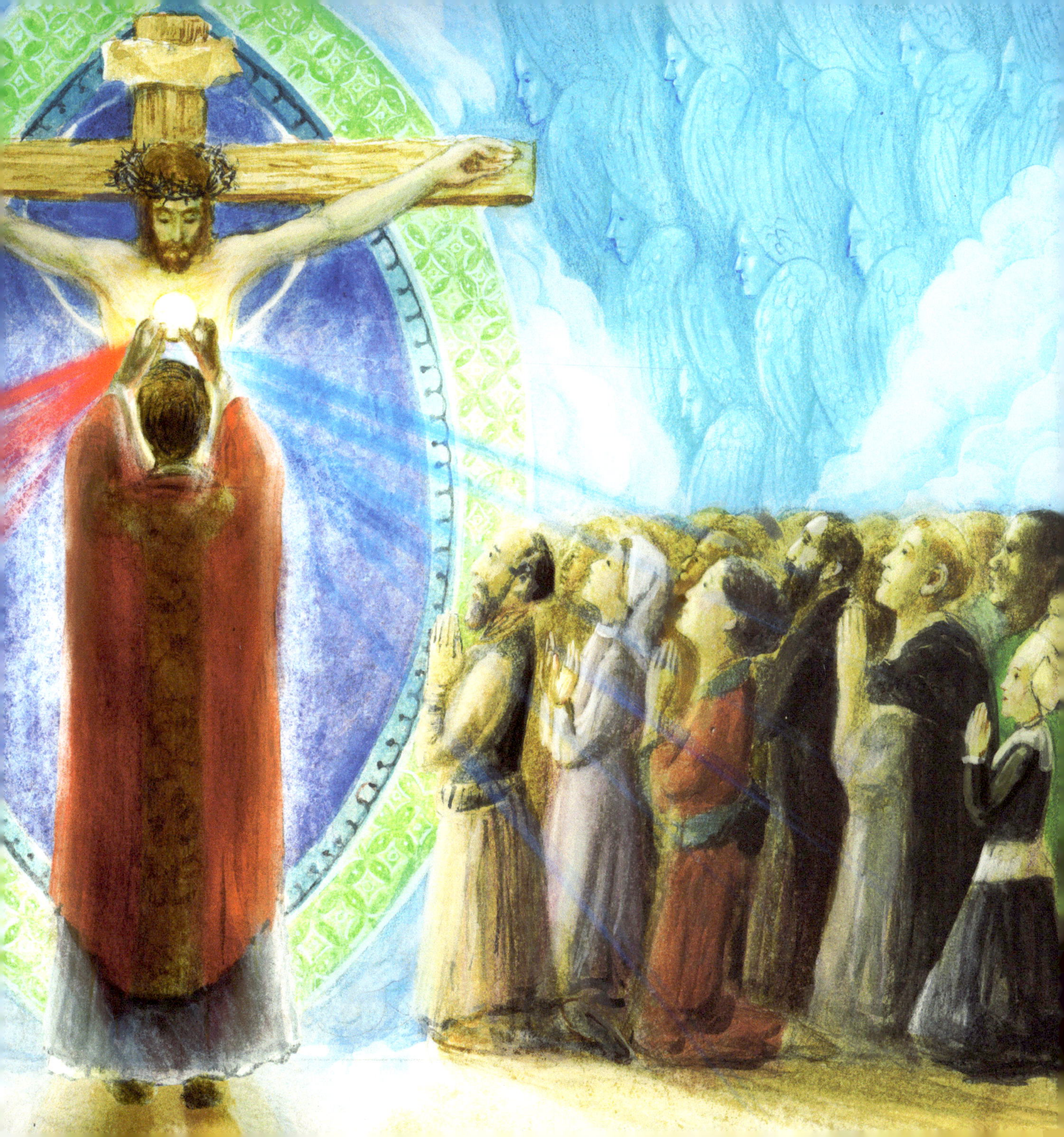

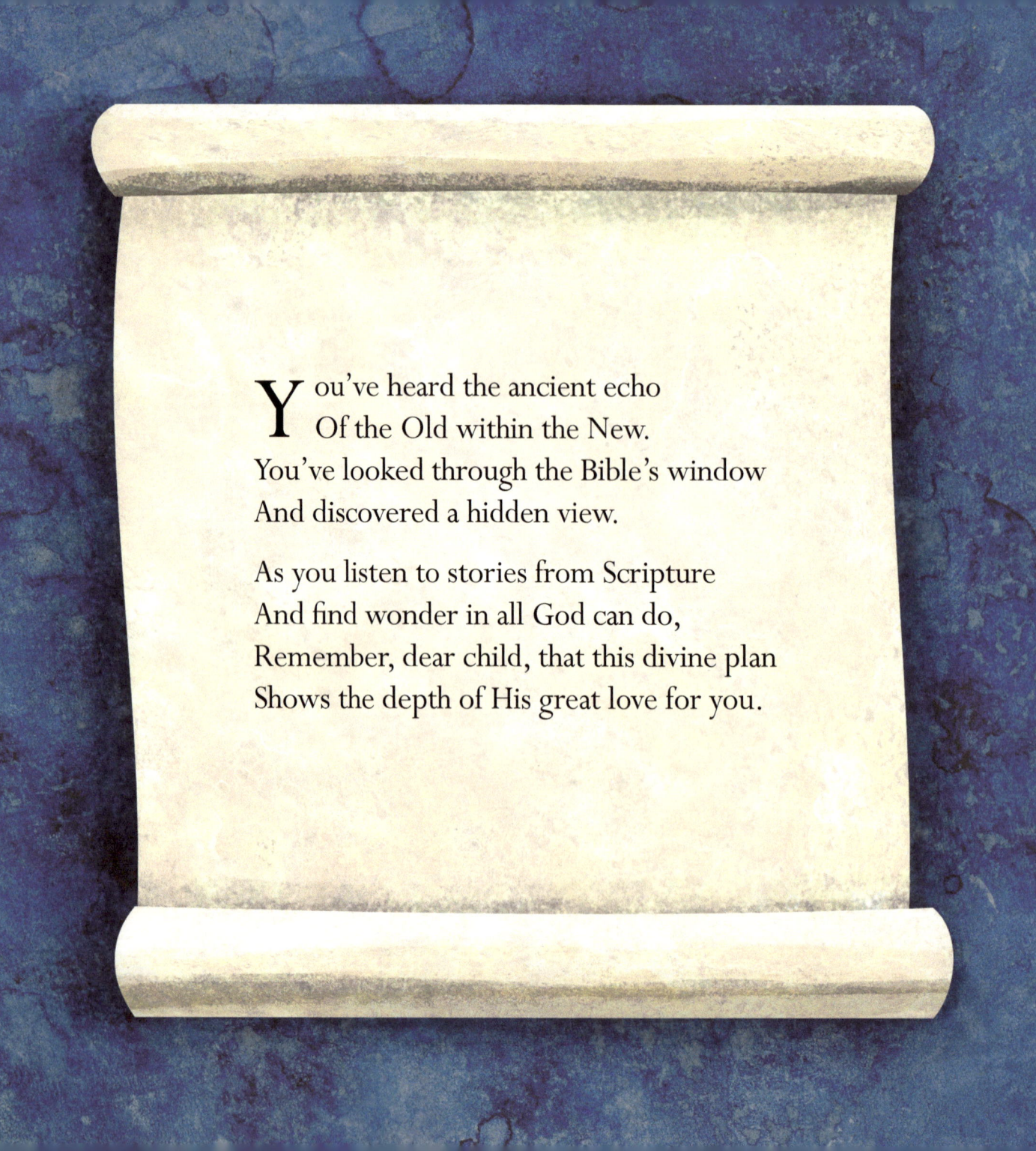

You've heard the ancient echo
 Of the Old within the New.
You've looked through the Bible's window
And discovered a hidden view.

As you listen to stories from Scripture
And find wonder in all God can do,
Remember, dear child, that this divine plan
Shows the depth of His great love for you.

Maura Roan McKeegan first learned about biblical typology when she was a graduate student in theology. As a school teacher, she believed that children would be as fascinated by the connections between the Old and New Testaments as she was—and that once they had the key, children could unlock countless hidden treasures in Scripture. This belief inspired her to write The Old and New Series of picture books, including the award-winning *The End of the Fiery Sword: Adam & Eve and Jesus & Mary* and *Into the Sea, Out of the Tomb: Jonah & Jesus*. She lives in Ohio with her husband, Shaun, and their four children.

Ted Schluenderfritz is the illustrator of several books including *A Life of Our Lord for Children*, *The Book of Angels*, and *Darby O'Gill and the Good People*. He is a freelance graphic designer and the art director for *Catholic Digest* and *Gilbert Magazine*. He lives in Littleton, Colorado with his wife Rachel and their six children. You can view more of his work at www.5sparrows.com.

More from the Old and New Series

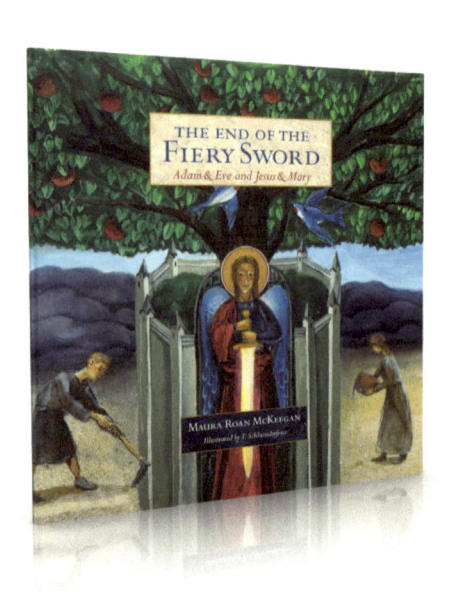

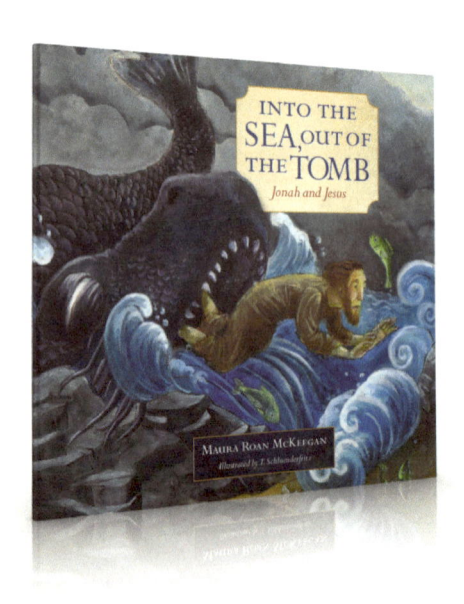

CPSIA information can be obtained
at www.ICGtesting.com
Printed in the USA
BVHW02n1022050418
512391BV00001B/13/P